THE HANDBOOK

Angela Hurd, Diana McQueen and Bob Boucher

The *Questions Publishing Company* Ltd
Birmingham
2005

The Questions Publishing Company Ltd
321 Bradford Street, Birmingham B5 6ET

© The Questions Publishing Company Ltd, 2005

First published in 2002

ISBN: 1 84190 095 8

Edited by Amanda Greenley
Designed by Al Stewart

Printed in the UK

CONTENTS

PREFACE

Welcome to SALLEY.

SALLEY stands for 'Structured Activities for Language and Literacy in the Early Years'.

SALLEY is a prevention intervention programme designed to teach phonological awareness skills (crucial skills for learning to read) to pre-school children in **any** setting.

SALLEY's primary aim is to enable and enhance the acquisition of literacy skills (i.e. to make it easier for children to learn to read and spell) through promoting phonological awareness skills.

You have purchased a toolkit including five pieces of equipment:

- The SALLEY handbook
- The SALLEY manual
- The SALLEY squirrel puppet
- The SALLEY video
- The SALLEY audio cassette

The handbook provides all the background information about the programme, including the research and statistics. The contents table will direct you to the sections which interest you most, however you are encouraged to read the handbook in its entirety in order to get 'best value' for you and your children.

The manual contains plans for 100 days of the structured intervention programme which can be delivered to groups or individuals to meet their specific needs. The manual contains all you need to get started.

The approach was developed in an inner city area, as a means of trying to prevent later literacy acquisition difficulties. It began its life as a structured intervention programme for children in their Nursery year, but has flourished into a comprehensive phonological awareness teaching package – which can be used with a range of children in a range of settings and be delivered by any pre-school practitioner.

The project has been presented publicly at several conferences including:

- The Royal College of Speech and Language Therapists' annual study day (McQueen, 1999)
- CPLOL Conference, Paris (Hurd and McQueen, 2000)
- The Royal College of Speech and Language Therapists' National Conference (Hurd and McQueen, 2001)
- The British Dyslexia Association National Conference (Hurd and McQueen, 2001)

A pleasing result has been the fostering of collaborative practice but most importantly the research outcomes have supported our initial hopes that the pre-school age group is more than ready for this type of intervention programme.

Angela Hurd, Diana McQueen, Bob Boucher, 2002

ACKNOWLEDGEMENTS

We would like to thank the following individuals and groups for their invaluable help and co-operation over the last five years, without which this project would not have been possible:

- The Head teachers, early years staff and pupils at the following Sandwell Metropolitan Borough Council schools who implemented the programme and enabled us to carry out pre- and post-programme testing:
  Brasshouse Infant School
  Cape Primary School
  Corbett Infant School
  Cronehills Primary School
  Devonshire Infant School
  Joseph Turner Primary School
  Jubilee Park Primary School
  St. Martin's C of E Primary School
  St. Paul's C of E Primary School
  Victoria Infant School
  Wednesbury Oak Primary School
- Phil Watts (Inclusion Support Manager/Principal Educational Psychologist) for his support for the venture and his efforts in securing funding through The Tipton Challenge and the Smethwick Single Regeneration Budget.
- Flis Parsons (Assistant Director of Primary Care, Sandwell Healthcare NHS Trust) who facilitated long term allocation of staff time.
- Julie Nettleton (Head of School of Speech and Language Therapy, at the University of Central England) who gave her support.
- Professor Rachel David (University of Central England) who gave much support and encouragement regarding the research design.

- Christine Molloy, Tracey Goodayle, Sunny Boparig, Emma Pontefract, Amber Elliot, and Nicola Saville, students from the University of Aston, who all assisted with testing and data analysis.
- Dr Saeed Haque (University of Central England) who gave advice about the statistical analysis.
- Rebecca Thirtle and Nayyar Areehy (Assistant Educational Psychologists) who carried out test and questionnaire administration.
- Linda Hisgett (SEN Advisory Teacher, Sandwell Child Psychology Service) who gave advice on the interpretation of the C.O.P.S results. Administration of the C.O.P.S assessment was carried out by Victoria Naylor.
- Linda Mann (Specialist Speech and Language Therapist, Sandwell Healthcare NHS Trust) who supported the programme throughout.
- Tracy Wilcock (Speech and Language Therapist, Solihull) who carried out the Edinburgh Articulation Test assessments.
- We would like to thank Stewart Ellis and Paul Turner for their technical expertise, and Mandy Payton for her help with typing.
- The SALLEY video was made with the help and co-operation of the pupils and staff at Princes End Primary School, Sandwell Metropolitan Borough Council. Thank you to Sandra Carter, Janet Orme, Elizabeth Allen and Katherine Lewis.
- The Makaton Vocabulary Development Project for permission to use their symbols for same/different as visual referents.

WHAT IS SO SPECIAL ABOUT
SALLEY?

Children normally enter the Nursery class during the year of their fourth birthday. By the time they reach the end of their Reception year (the year of their fifth birthday) we expect them to be able to "read a range of familiar and common words and simple sentences independently" and to "use their phonic knowledge to write simple regular words and make phonetically plausible attempts at more complex words". (Curriculum Guidance for the Foundation Stage: DfEE 2000).

There can be little argument with the view that a child's ability to acquire literacy skills is closely linked to his/her language skills. Locke, Ginsborg and Peers (2002) report that "there is substantial evidence to show that spoken and written language share some processes in common and that the development of literacy is supported by the development of spoken language". Their research found that more than half of the children from areas of poverty were language delayed, and this resonates with the findings from the SALLEY study (see page 51 onwards).

Research has highlighted the particular importance of one aspect of language, namely **phonological awareness** in the development of literacy. Children with well developed phonological awareness skills have knowledge of the constituent sounds which make up words, and the ability to manipulate these sounds at will.

If the acquisition of literacy skills can be significantly enhanced by phonological awareness skills then it is imperative that early years practitioners are able to provide children with the necessary learning experiences that will promote the development of these skills. The provision of the necessary learning experiences will need to draw on a sound knowledge of child development, learning theory, and language development, particularly the development of phonological awareness skills. All of these need to be incorporated into a carefully structured and planned approach to teaching.

SALLEY fulfils all of these requirements and does so through a set of principles that make it applicable to all children regardless of their age, ethnicity, social background, and previously acquired skills.

These principles are summarised below. SALLEY:

- does not assume any prior knowledge is in place.
- allows for individual rates of learning (differentiation).
- has phonological awareness as its primary focus because of the proven link between phonological awareness and literacy acquisition.
- has identified five 'core' skills which are essential for any learning, not just language learning.
- teaches those core skills, which are learned, thereby allowing equal access to the programme for children who, pre-nursery, have not been exposed to a conducive environment.
- teaches the key language concepts that are necessary for children to acquire phonological awareness (i.e. a safety net for children whose early language environment has not enabled the learning of such abstract vocabulary).
- follows the developmental sequence of skills acquisition, rather than tying in age levels to expected/anticipated National Curriculum guidelines.
- focuses almost entirely on the input loop.
- is multi-sensory. It involves looking, listening and doing. This is the way that young children learn. It is the stage before more formal education when 'listening and responding' are the norm.

- uses visual referents and provides all the clues a child needs to successfully complete a task through use of gesture, intonation and facial expression on the part of the adult delivering the programme, and then allows for the phased withdrawal of these prompts as the children become more confident.
- uses pure phonics.
- involves errorless learning. Clues given are gradually withdrawn, rather than the learning objectives being delivered at a higher level, the child experiencing failure, and the adult having to 'back track' and try to ascertain the point of breakdown.
- uses recurrent themes.
- can be used on a daily basis in a way that makes it part of the normal nursery routine.
- can be used with groups or individuals.
- can be delivered by any childcare practitioner.
- can be used in early education in a preventative way.

SALLEY DOES NOT ASSUME ANY PRIOR KNOWLEDGE IS IN PLACE

What do we mean by 'prior knowledge'?

When children enter one of a variety of pre-school settings (day nursery, play group, nursery school, etc) at the Foundation Stage, they bring with them a wide variety of skills, aptitudes, and experiences. Some will have well developed expressive and receptive language skills; will have enjoyed a rich variety of experiences; participated in activities with friends and family; had wide exposure to books and the media; and a wealth of opportunity to experience toys and games. Other children arrive with an extremely poor understanding of spoken language and under-developed ability to express themselves; restricted experiences; socio-economic and emotional difficulties; and a limited range of play opportunities. Locke et al (2002) found that in a study of 223 children raised in poverty more than half were language delayed, in contrast to having cognitive skills that fell within the normal range. In summary, children arrive in their pre-school settings with differing amounts of 'prior knowledge'.

SALLEY is designed to meet the needs of all children and follows a developmental sequence. It is therefore important that the programme should start at a point that takes account of a wide and differing range of experience and abilities. This means starting at the beginning and assuming no prior knowledge. All children can participate from the beginning of SALLEY. By so doing there is little chance of failure with the higher order skills as they are not built on unreliable or non-existent foundations.

Will the more able children get bored?

At the start of the programme, when the core skills are introduced, some children will have no difficulty participating in the activities and will provide good models for others in the group who have less experience and lower abilities. Experience has shown that even if a particular skill is well developed, children enjoy practising that skill, and get a sense of achievement by repeated successful completion of a task. All children enjoy practitioner approval gained through responding appropriately to an instruction.

In summary, regardless of what the child brings to the pre-school setting, SALLEY makes no assumptions about them, begins at the beginning, and takes them step by step through the programme, thus ensuring successful learning for all.

SALLEY ALLOWS FOR INDIVIDUAL RATES OF LEARNING (DIFFERENTIATION)

What do we mean by differentiation? Basically, differentiation means that each child is treated as an individual. Within the context of the programme, individual learning styles and rates of learning are recognised and catered for. Successful differentiation is easily achieved when working with individuals and small groups.

The Qualifications and Curriculum Authority (2000) point out that it is most important for children to develop "positive attitudes and dispositions towards their learning". This can only be achieved in an environment of success, praise and reinforcement where children develop confidence in their own abilities.

A key means of ensuring that this happens is to guarantee that individual differences can be supported within a structured, planned approach. It may be, for example, that most of the children have reached the stage of successfully selecting a given letter sound from a choice of four. However, there may be one child who can only achieve success if the choice of letter sounds presented is limited to two.

The observation skills of the practitioner are brought into play here. That child would participate in the same task but with a reduced number of cards appropriate to his/her particular needs.

Meeting the needs of the individual is possible when a wide range of teaching strategies are used. SALLEY uses a variety of different teaching techniques, including the multi-sensory approach, recurrent themes and errorless learning. This ensures that there is something to meet the needs of all children, no matter what their race, gender or disability.

As SALLEY relies almost entirely on the input loop, children with English as an additional language can take part on an equal footing because the teaching and learning is consistently supported by visual referents and non-verbal cues.

Clearly, many children learn the same things in different ways, and at different rates. SALLEY aims to make it easy for practitioners to apply their skills of differentiation within the context of small group or individual work.

SALLEY's PRIMARY FOCUS IS
PHONOLOGICAL AWARENESS

What do we mean by 'phonological awareness'?

Phonological awareness is central to SALLEY. The DfEE (1998) define it as "awareness of sounds within words – demonstrated, for example, by the ability to generate rhyme, alliteration and in segmenting and blending compound sounds". All these skills have direct relevance to the acquisition of literacy.

Many children with decoding problems have been hampered in reading "because they are unable to generalise from one word to another" (Reid, 1998). It is crucial, therefore, to teach sounds/phonemes. Reid (1998) goes as far as to say that "beginning readers should receive some structured training in grapheme/phoneme correspondence".

The primary aim of SALLEY is to promote the development of phonological awareness, which has been identified by many researchers as closely linked to the development of literacy. Some researchers feel that there is a 'cause and effect' relationship with literacy. Given that literacy is of prime importance, **any** skills which can so strongly influence its development should be given serious consideration.

Within SALLEY the primary focus is on the 'input loop' (see page 26). This facilitates participation by younger, shyer and less able children, and ensures that group work is a positive experience for all children.

Where does SALLEY start?

Initially, children are introduced to individual letters and their corresponding sounds. The ability to relate a sound to its 'visual referent', i.e. the grapheme, can be acquired surprisingly quickly by all children. LeProvost (1999) found that babies with Down's Syndrome could easily discriminate letter/sound cards.

In the first dew days of the programme, children are gradually and systematically introduced to a range of letters and their corresponding sounds. These are slowly increased, with lots of time given to providing multiple opportunities for revision and repetition.

In order that all children can achieve this recurring learning objective, the task is presented in a variety of different ways (see pages 28 and 37).

Why is phonological awareness so important?

Goswami and Bryant (1990) present a very detailed overview of research that has been done in the field. Suffice it to say that "the centrality of phonological awareness to the development of efficient written language skills has been demonstrated through a range of studies" (Layton and Deeny, 1996).

Adams (1990) found four key tasks could predict reading skill:

1. Syllable and phoneme segmentation: counting out or identifying the constituent syllable and/or phonemes within words (Lieberman, Shankweiler, Fischer and Carter, 1974).

2. Phoneme manipulation tasks which require the child to delete, add or transpose phonemes within words (Lundberg, Frost and Peterson, 1988), and explicit awareness of the onset/rime division (Goswami and Bryant, 1990).
3. Sound blending tasks in which the child is asked to put sounds together (Perfetti, Bell, Beck and Hughes, 1987).
4. Rhyming tasks which include knowledge of nursery rhymes (Maclean, Bryant and Bradley, 1987) and the identification of the 'odd word out', i.e. non-rhyming word, in a sequence of three words (Sound categorisation test: Bradley and Bryant, 1985).

In addition, all children need to develop the ability to reflect on their language (meta-linguistic skills). This allows children to know cognitively:

- which bits rhyme and why (rather than just recite a list or rhyme), and
- which words in a list are the odd ones out because they do not follow the rhyming pattern (i.e. rhyme/ no rhyme), for example.

SALLEY ensures that all children learn the vocabulary for talking about spoken language and the constituents of individual words, by teaching key language concepts (see page 22). Interestingly, the development of meta-linguistic skills has been shown to be more advanced in the child who is bilingual because they are more aware of the structure of language generally (see page 48).

The SALLEY programme carefully builds up children's phonological awareness skills by following the developmental sequence and ensuring that all new skills are built on strong foundations.

SALLEY IDENTIFIES FIVE
CORE SKILLS

What do we mean by 'core skills'?

These are skills that are pre-requisites for the acquisition of higher order skills.

Within the SALLEY programme, **5 skills** are identified as being central to **any** learning, not just language learning.

The SALLEY core skills are:

- Attention
- Listening
- Memory
- Discrimination
- Sequencing

All these are **learned** skills.

They are all important in a variety of learning situations across **all** aspects of the Curriculum. One could consider the importance of sequencing in both maths and reading, discrimination in spelling tasks, and memory in successful task completion in science, for example.

Consider how often the following instructions might be used within the early years learning environment:

- "I want you to listen carefully..."
- "Pay attention now..."
- "Remember..."
- "This is different to/from..."
- "Think about what happened before..."
- "What comes/came next...?"

All these instructions are part of the daily teaching and learning environment in Nurseries and Reception classes nationwide. Their success depends upon a level of understanding and compliance, which is largely assumed.

Think how some children might feel faced with instructions using this kind of vocabulary!

So, what do we mean by...

Attention: the ability to take notice of, and learn from what we see and hear going on around us. This leads to sustained attention, i.e. concentration, which is crucial for learning.

Cooper, Moodley and Reynell (1978) identified task-focussed stages in the development of attention skills. We have summarised their ideas here, but for further information please refer to *Helping Children's Language Development*.

STAGE 1 (up to 1 year)	a) pays fleeting attention, but is highly distractible b) attention is directed to an explorative activity
STAGE 2 (up to 2 years)	a) attention is held rigidly by own choice of activity b) no tolerance of adult interference in task
STAGE 3 (up to 3 years)	a) single channel attention, attends to adult choice of activity b) ability to adapt to adult's directions emerges c) needs help transferring attention focus to directions of task
STAGE 4 (up to 4 years)	a) begins slowly to control own attention focus b) moves towards looking at speaker only when instructions become difficult
STAGE 5 (4–5 years)	Integrated auditory and visual attention for short spells
STAGE 6 (5 years +)	Well integrated and sustained attention

Their work is invaluable in helping us to understand that attention skills cannot just be "expected", but have to be learned.

Listening: more than just hearing sounds, it involves being able, over time, to understand and interpret them too.

Memory: (auditory memory is particularly important in SALLEY) to store and recall increasing amounts of information in order to be able to act upon it. Reid (1998) states that the child with dyslexic difficulties may have difficulty in remembering, retaining and recalling information.

Discrimination: (auditory discrimination is a crucial part of SALLEY) to perceive and interpret the differences between sounds on a variety of levels. Research findings have indicated a link between some aspects of auditory perception and the presence of dyslexia (Masterson, Hazan and Wijayatilake, 1995; Tallal, 1980). Vance (1994) identifies that many children with literacy difficulties misperceive words. The same researcher states that in-put processing skills play a vital role in the development of phonological representations.

Sequencing: to recall and produce information in the right order. Sequencing skills require reliable memory skills. Bishop (1997) states that the child who encodes incoming stimuli rapidly and efficiently will have time to refresh the traces of stimuli earlier in the series, however the child who takes much longer at the encoding process will have little spare capacity for rehearsal. This deficit is evident in children with dyslexia and specific language impairment.

In SALLEY 'good listening' is introduced from day one. It is an end point reached via 'good sitting' and 'good looking'. Behavioural activities are used to demonstrate and work towards the abstract concept of what constitutes 'good listening'.

SALLEY TEACHES THE KEY LANGUAGE CONCEPTS

What do we mean by 'key language concepts'?

SALLEY uses the term 'key language concepts' to mean knowledge of specific **words** (or concepts), used to teach children the content of the programme. Children need to **understand** what these key words mean in order to access phonological awareness.

This idea is not new! All teaching relies upon the learner's ability to understand the language used. Bishop (1997) states that to some extent the task of language learning is to "map words onto pre-existing non verbal concepts". In keeping with the SALLEY philosophy that nothing is 'assumed' to be in place, these key concepts are actively taught prior to children being expected to use them to tackle phonological awareness tasks later in the programme.

The SALLEY key language concepts are:

- Same/different
- Long/short
- Silly/sensible (for real/non-words)
- Rhyme/no rhyme
- Beginning/end

The key language concepts are tools added to the SALLEY toolbox. Children learn them, become familiar with them and can ultimately use them to tackle new and increasingly complex tasks. The aim being that no child is disadvantaged at the outset.

Many of these concepts are considered by the authors to be 'difficult' because of their abstract nature.

- "Find me something that begins with the **same** sound."
- "Which one is **different?**"
- "Which sound comes at the **end?**"
- "Which ones **rhyme?**"
- "Find me another **long** sound."
- "Can you clap **your** name?" (Syllable sorting)

If a child fails, how can we know whether the task is too difficult, or whether the language used is unfamiliar? The reader is invited to consider the complexities of language used in any teaching situation, and the impact it may have on children's outcomes.

For many children, particularly those from disadvantaged backgrounds, the 'tools' must be in the box if progress is to be made. SALLEY aims to do this.

SALLEY FOLLOWS THE
DEVELOPMENTAL SEQUENCE

What is the developmental sequence and why is it important?

Many studies have looked at the development of language in children – in fact its study forms a whole academic research area in its own right. What is evident is that whilst all children display individual differences there is a clearly defined route along which language develops. Thus, a developmental sequence has been identified that applies across all languages.

Knowing what this sequence is, allows the practitioner to identify children who have communication needs and enables them to take appropriate action to help children reach their full potential.

The development of phonological awareness builds on the foundations of spoken language and also follows a developmental sequence. For example, it is very difficult for children to identify rhyming pairs when they cannot discriminate sound shakers, yet little time is currently spent teaching the prerequisite skills before children are exposed to the demands of the literacy hour. This means that many children are disadvantaged because they have not had the opportunity to develop a strong foundation before they are presented with tasks that are too difficult for them. What is needed is input geared to the child's developmental level and opportunities for learning within the pre-school setting.

The DfEE have laid out a number of key principles for early years education in their recent publication *Curriculum Guidance for the Foundation Stage* (DfEE, 2000). These principles include:

"Effective education requires practitioners who understand that children develop rapidly during the early years - physically, intellectually, emotionally, and socially. Children are entitled to provision that supports and extends knowledge and skills, understanding and confidence, and helps them to overcome any disadvantage."

"Practitioners must be able to observe and respond appropriately to children, informed by a knowledge of how children develop and learn and a clear understanding of possible next steps in their development and learning."

Interestingly these principles are not always found in pre-school settings (Ofsted, 1998).

SALLEY offers the practitioner a structured programme that follows the developmental sequence for teaching phonological awareness skills. It serves two functions. It allows for the early identification of children who are struggling, and ensures that the practitioner knows what to do next in terms of formulating early learning goals to facilitate learning in this area.

SALLEY FOCUSES ON THE INPUT LOOP

What do we mean by 'the input loop'?

The notion of having input versus output comes from the psycholinguistic approach as a means of conceptualising children's speech processing ability. Stackhouse and Wells (1997) have written widely in this field, pointing out that speech processing skills play a major role in the development of reading and spelling. They show in their diagram that both looking and listening are important on the input side for developing lexical representations. Basically, this means being able to understand what has been read (decode) and then, on the output side, being able to spell (encode).

This is well explained by Stackhouse and Wells (1997). We have represented their ideas here, but further information can be found in their book.

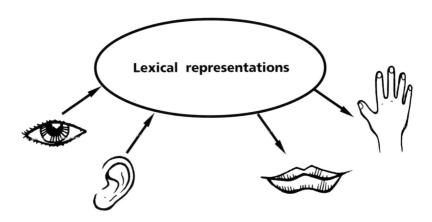

The basic structure of the speech processing and literacy system: Stackhouse and Wells (1997).

Clearly the aim is to foster the development of representations and 'move down' the model, developing output (or encoding) skills. However, as many of the children who can benefit from SALLEY are young, or may have specific difficulties in these areas, the focus of the programme is on input.

This means that children are asked to point, give or show, rather than verbally respond. Again, this gives equal access to children, who, for one reason or another, may be reluctant to participate orally.

A variety of different input tasks are finely graded to promote development within the programme. These begin with work on auditory discrimination, e.g. post the one that begins with /b/ from a choice of two. This is a critical skill for children with language disorder and/or dyslexia (Merzenich, Jenkins and Johnston, 1996). The programme moves on to use a variety of listening and discrimination tasks which gradually build up to focus on the identification of rhyme.

Tasks include real and non-word listening tasks, sound shakers, picture/object selection, same/different discrimination tasks, work on onset/coda (the consonants preceding the rhyme are the 'onset' and the consonants following the vowel are the 'coda'), rhyme judgements, rhyme detection, decoding of a sequence of sounds and silent sorting tasks. See the manual for more detail and the developmental sequence used in SALLEY.

Using this framework also allows for the identification of children who are experiencing specific problems in any one area. This can be particularly useful in trying to decide where some children may need extra help and allows the practitioner to direct specific work to meet individual needs. This can be used to focus very specifically on core areas of need in children with dyslexia.

SALLEY IS MULTI-SENSORY

Another of the key teaching principles used in SALLEY is the multi-sensory approach. This is a very common teaching method, widely used in special education, which has equal application to **all** children.

What do we mean by 'multi-sensory'?

It works by tapping into all the senses which promote learning. The visual and auditory senses (looking and listening) tend to dominate teaching, however there are other senses which are crucial in helping children make sense of the environment. Some are very evident in the learning of babies and young children, for example, olfactory (smell) and tactile (touch). These tend to be superseded as maturation occurs but are still used by us all when encountering new learning experiences. Proprioception (position in space) and the kinaesthetic sense (movement) also have a continuing role to play in helping young children build a store of learned items.

SALLEY aims to make as much use of input modalities as possible.

Why use the multi-sensory approach?

Various essential elements are identified for successful teaching and learning:

- over learning and automaticity,
- a highly structured approach, and
- a sequential and cumulative approach.

These are all found in SALLEY. "The multi-sensory methods utilise all available senses simultaneously" (Reid, 1998). With the aim of facilitating literacy development in mind, Ellis (1991) points out "in reading, a number of cognitive skills such as memory and visual auditory and oral skills interact". It is important, therefore, to build on these skills as early as possible. "If the learner has a difficulty in dealing with information by way of the auditory channel then this could, perhaps, be compensated for through the use of the visual channel". (Reid, 1998).

SALLEY includes tasks that use all the senses to help children remember things. In dealing with mixed groups of children, this facilitates the best way of enhancing individual learning styles, to get the 'best fit' on an individual basis. Very young children often respond best to tactile and kinaesthetic approaches and will need help to benefit from visual and auditory input. Children are encouraged to touch and feel, by holding objects and touching letter sound cards throughout. The senses of movement and position in space (kinaesthetic and proprioceptive) are embedded in copying and sequencing body movements. These feature in the early stages of the programme and are re-visited, both in the original form and via posting and positioning of letter sound cards. Movement, as part of the learning process, has been found to promote memory development, and that, in turn, furthers learning.

SALLEY offers a combination of approaches to meet the needs of the individual in the learning process.

The multi-sensory approach is so much a part of SALLEY that it is embedded throughout. From the outset, children are introduced to visual referents (pictures/symbols) that support the understanding of the concepts and enable the development of meta-linguistic skills. This continues with the introduction of letter shapes (phoneme/grapheme correspondence).

Multi-sensory strategies are currently widely used in teaching dyslexic children. However, by the time children are identified as having dyslexia they are viewed as failures of the teaching and learning system. A multi-sensory approach aims to prevent these potential failures. The SALLEY multi-sensory philosophy enables all children to access the programme equally.

Multi-sensory strategies have been found to benefit learners of all ages because they find the input mode of 'best fit'.

SALLEY USES VISUAL REFERENTS

What do we mean by 'visual referents'?

Visual referents are tangible representations of abstract concepts. One of the key teaching principles of SALLEY is the use of visual referents because these are designed to aid teaching and learning and support the traditional auditory approach.

Visual referents are crucial in ensuring that children acquire the full meaning of key language concepts used in the programme. SALLEY resources provide visual referents to support several complex and abstract concepts which are difficult to explain to children of differing abilities but which are needed to enable children to develop meta-linguistic skills. These include:

- Same/different
- Long/short
- Silly/sensible
- Rhyme/no rhyme

Why use visual referents?

Visual referents have consistently been shown to benefit children by promoting very early access to literacy. This is because "literacy can basically be seen on a representational continuum from very early object use to the manipulation of letters to produce words and sentences" (Williams, 2002). Thus, visual referents make spoken language more tangible and help children's memory development, thereby promoting learning.

As the eventual aim is literacy development, visual referents also promote the understanding of representations. After all, text is just another form of representation. Visual referents also have 'iconicity', i.e. the picture may look like the thing it represents, unlike the spoken word (Light, Remington, Clarke and Watson, 1989).

The use of visual referents in SALLEY

These are used throughout SALLEY. Children are introduced to visual referents from the outset when key language concepts are introduced (e.g. long/short). They are then modified and extended to include pairing of the picture/symbol with the spoken word, for more complex concepts needed to talk about sounds and their properties.

One of the main benefits of visual referent use is that children can indicate their understanding by pointing to the picture/symbol rather than having to say anything.

The SALLEY research shows that for more than 60% of children, visual referents achieved the following:

- provided a concrete representation of a concept,
- described a concept, not just a word,
- promoted attention and listening (there is something to look at as well as listen to),
- aided the development of representation skills generally (important for literacy acquisition),
- allowed children to demonstrate understanding without saying anything, and
- helped foster learning for less able children (as part of the multi-sensory approach).

The symbols used in SALLEY have been taken from those used by the Makaton Vocabulary Development Project.

SALLEY USES PURE PHONICS

What are 'pure phonics' and what do they have to do with SALLEY?

The concept of 'pure phonics' may already be familiar. In the context of SALLEY however, pure phonics refers to how the individual/initial letter sounds are introduced/articulated.

Individual letter sounds are introduced and reinforced. Sounds are analysed according to their 'qualities' (Dean, Howell, Hill and Waters, 1990).

You will find visual referents within the tool kit for 'long' and 'short' concepts. These visual referents refer to different qualities of sounds (initial letter sounds).

The reader's attention is drawn to the grid at the end of this section which identifies sounds on the basis of 'quality'.

- Long sounds – this refers to any sound which can be prolonged or **stretched** when articulated. For example:

  /f/, /s/, /h/, /v/, /z/, /m/, /n/, /r/, /y/, /l/, /w/

- Short sounds – this refers to any sound which **stands alone** and should **not** be followed by /uh/ when articulated alone. For example:

  /p/, /b/, /t/, /d/, /k/(/c/), /g/

Why is this important?

Readers will remember that SALLEY is primarily an **input** programme (i.e. children have to say very little, but they **do** have to participate in sound imitation).

From the beginning, if pure phonics are used, children will

be eased into the crucial skill of 'phonic blending' without the trauma of having to **unlearn** the additional /uh/ at the end of both long and short sounds. Many children do **not** learn to blend efficiently because they have learnt initial letter sounds with the added /uh/.

As an example, readers are asked to consider the following sequence of letter sounds:

m—a—n

Without pure phonics this can be manifest as:

Muh—an—nuh = muhanuh

With pure phonics this is manifest as:

Mmmm(long)—a(short)—nnnn(long) = man

SALLEY advocates pure phonics right from the beginning as the right way to introduce children to learning initial letter sounds.

Long sounds	/f/, /v/, /s/, /z/, /h/, /m/, /n/, /r/, /l/ /y/ (begins as /ee/) /w/ (begins as /oo/)
Short sounds	/p/, /b/, /t/, /d/, /k/ (/c/), /g/ and vowels /a/ /e/ /i/ /o/ /u/
Oddities (combinations of more than one sound)	/j/ (/d/ + /y/) /q/ (/k/ + /w/) /x/ (/e/ + /k/ + /s/)

How can pure phonics help?

Using long and short sounds helps children by:

- aiding their short-term auditory memory, and
- ultimately facilitating blending.

SALLEY USES ERRORLESS LEARNING

What is 'errorless learning'?

Errorless learning allows the child to succeed **every** time. There are multiple positive benefits for both children and practitioners: increased self-esteem and motivation, maintenance of interest and effective use of time. A positive atmosphere is created in the classroom, by building on the children's strengths, supporting their weaknesses and increasing their self-esteem.

The term comes from an area of psychology known as applied behavioural analysis. The practitioner either shows or tells the child how to respond to a demand and thereby allows the child to respond correctly and avoid making errors.

In errorless learning the child is always right because they always makes the correct response. When the practitioner makes a demand, he/she has to make a very quick judgement as to whether the child is going to make the correct response or not. If the child falters in response, then the practitioner quickly steps in and offers a prompt, either gestural or verbal, before the child is able to make a mistake. This means that the child, with the help of the prompt, is able to make the correct response. The period of time between the practitioner asking the question and giving a prompt should be no more than two seconds.

The practitioner will follow the correct response with praise, thereby providing positive reinforcement and increasing the chances of successful repetition. What is important is that the child arrives at the correct response either independently or with practitioner intervention through adequate prompts (Heckerman, Alber, Hooper and Heward, 1998).

Children who are taught through errorless learning do not make judgements about the perceived ease or difficulty of tasks. The easy ones are those that can be completed independently and receive positive reinforcement; the difficult ones are those which require prompting and which **also** receive positive reinforcement. The experience of failure is potentially damaging for all children. This is why SALLEY aims to build on success.

SALLEY USES RECURRENT THEMES

What are 'recurrent themes'?
Why are they important for SALLEY?

The SALLEY programme has a tiered approach to the introduction, practice and use of:

- core skills,
- key language concepts, and
- phonological awareness skills.

These three main areas are **'themes'**.
As described in each section in *The Handbook*:

- **core skills** are essential for any kind of learning.
- **key language concepts** are essential if children are to understand the language used in the programme and have the vocabulary for talking about language.
- **phonological awareness skills** lead to enhanced literacy acquisition.

These three main themes are constantly re-visited (i.e. are recurrent) throughout the programme.

As the programme progresses, children are able to apply their learned core skills, in combination with the key language concepts, to tackle phonological awareness tasks.

The 'themes' are tools in the SALLEY toolkit. As with any learning situation, revision and opportunity to practise lead to familiarity, fluency and the confidence to ultimately use the SALLEY 'tools' spontaneously and creatively to perform increasingly more complex tasks.

This approach accommodates:

- the slower learner who requires lots of revision,
- the absentee whose needs cannot always be catered for,
- the child who has English as an additional language,
- the 'quiet' child who may not demonstrate their knowledge/ability before the opportunity has passed,
- the 'average' child whose confidence thrives with familiarity.

This idea is not new! **Any** learning opportunity benefits from revision and the opportunity to practise skills learned. The difference with SALLEY is that 'revision' is in-built and not a random or 'ad hoc' arrangement. Hence the concept of **'recurrent themes'**.

SALLEY CAN BE USED AS PART OF THE DAILY ROUTINE

A typical SALLEY teaching session would involve:

- one SALLEY-trained staff member working with a group of up to 10 children in an area suitable for small group activities.
- working through a programme of 5/6 activities in the order given.
- a duration of no more than 20 minutes.

Detailed information on running the sessions is provided in the manual.

SALLEY CAN BE USED WITH GROUPS AND INDIVIDUALS

SALLEY can be used equally well with groups or individuals. When using SALLEY in groups, as a preventative intervention, mixed ability groups are recommended. This is because they not only reflect the learning style within the early years curriculum, but also the wider ethos of both social and educational inclusion.

- Confident children are used to demonstrate the material, and new items as they arise.
- Less able children have the opportunity to learn by the example of their peers.
- Lots of rehearsal takes place.
- The programme allows for differentiation on a daily basis.
- Group learning is also a social experience: it allows for turn-taking, repetition, peer support and the celebration of success as a group.

SALLEY can also be used as a 'treatment' or recovery intervention.

It is possible to pull out certain SALLEY tasks for individual or very small group remediation if necessary.

Why and when might this occur?

- At Reception age, groups of children requiring additional help in some/all areas of phonological awareness (see page 46).
- Older children, in very small groups or individually, who may have been identified as dyslexic or 'at risk' of dyslexia (see page 50).
- Children with learning difficulties who may need extra time, repetition and revision (see page 46).

SALLEY CAN BE DELIVERED BY ANY CHILDCARE PRACTITIONER

Teachers, SENCos, nursery nurses, learning support practitioners and speech and language therapists were all involved in the original research. The potential list is much greater: it may also be appropriate to include child-minders for example. SALLEY is a multi-disciplinary tool, and can be delivered by **any** responsible adult involved in the care and education of pre-school children.

The teaching of literacy skills has traditionally been the role of teachers. Until comparatively recently, phonological awareness has been the province of speech and language therapists working to remediate speech out-put problems.

Less well known or understood, perhaps, is the role that speech and language therapists have in written language disorders. Guidelines for good working practice with written language disorders are laid down by the speech and language therapists' professional body. Locke et al (2002) state that an inclusive approach is needed, so that spoken language skills and literacy development are supported in pre-school settings.

The preparation for reading readiness involves providing children with the opportunity to acquire and develop a range of skills. These opportunities are made available through a range of activities in both childcare and early years settings, and in the context of the SALLEY programme can be delivered by **any** and **all** the staff in those settings.

SALLEY aims to provide pre-literacy hour opportunities in a complete package to prepare children for reading readiness. It is available to any early years practitioner, in any pre-school setting: educational, independent or social services based.

SALLEY operates from the premise that teaching phonological awareness skills is the joint and shared responsibility of us all!

SALLEY CAN BE USED IN A PREVENTATIVE WAY

What do we mean by 'preventative'?

SALLEY can be used successfully as an early intervention programme. "Research has established that human development is most rapid in the pre-school years" (Abudarham, 2002). Thus it is most important where there is a possibility of later difficulties, that intervention is directed primarily between the ages of 0 and 6 (Abudarham, 2002). In fact Karnes and Lee (1978) have noted that "only through early identification and appropriate programming can children develop their potential". Layton and Deeny in 1996 pointed out how important it was for pre-school children to be trained in the skills which support alphabetic literacy development. After much work in the field, they conclude "we remain convinced that children's phonological skills should be examined in the early years, before the beginning of formal literacy instruction". They also point out that by running programmes, such as SALLEY for example, "children with a disposition towards literacy difficulties, arising in connection with phonological weakness, can be identified and provided with the type of enrichment which can nurture prerequisite skills". Similar sentiments are expressed by Locke et al (2002). They note that in other countries "children are helped to understand rhyme and word structure". In addition, children are encouraged to develop their auditory memory, and skills are carefully targeted with the emphasis on the **practitioner** fostering learning.

In what sense is SALLEY preventative?

SALLEY was born out of a professional concern for the way in which many of our Key Stage 1 pupils were seen to be failing in their attempts to master early literacy skills. Multi-disciplinary meetings about how these children might be helped highlighted a need for something that provided the children with a firm foundation in language and particularly in phonological awareness skills. In many cases the need was for underpinning foundations; what SALLEY refers to as the 'core skills'.

Professional boundaries cease to exist when the child is placed at the centre. The teaching of literacy has traditionally been seen as the teacher's role and the teaching of phonological awareness that of the speech and language therapist. However these are false divisions. Overall a developmental approach, through use of a structured programme of activities based on firm theoretical principles and delivered on a daily basis, is what children need, and with such young children an errorless learning approach is also key.

What do they do in successful educational systems abroad?

The idea of prevention is reflected in Europe where comparative studies have pinpointed the features of pre-school education systems in the most successful countries, for example Hungary. During the pre-school years, the educational focus is based on developing the following key areas (upon which the later formal teaching is based):

- attention, listening, memory and meta-linguistic skills,
- group working skills, and

- conceptual understanding and the development of spoken language.

Teaching is highly structured and moves slowly to allow consolidation of tangible concepts.

The majority of the distinguishing features of these successful pre-school systems can be found in SALLEY. SALLEY cannot change the statutory demands made on our schools, but using it at the Foundation Stage will provide one piece of a jigsaw that could prevent many children from failure in literacy.

WHICH CHILDREN WILL BENEFIT FROM SALLEY?

SALLEY can be used with a variety of child populations:

All pre-school settings
The programme was originally designed for all children attending mainstream nursery classes, i.e. the year during which the children have their fourth birthday. There are, of course, many different establishments where young children of this age can be found: local authority nurseries, nursery centres, playgroups, pre-schools, accredited child-minders in approved child-minding networks, or schools in the independent, private or voluntary sectors, and maintained schools. All children can benefit regardless of their gender, age, ethnicity, socio-economic background or general ability.

Reception classes
Children in their Reception year can benefit from SALLEY, particularly those who are not felt to be ready for the introduction of the teaching of phonics. During the research stage of the scheme, many schools requested the SALLEY programme and materials. A number of Reception teachers were well aware that many of their children were not ready or adequately prepared for the demands of the literacy hour (DfEE, 1998), so they needed a programme that led in to this. SALLEY provides the necessary foundations and teaches the fundamental principles necessary.

Children with learning difficulties
SALLEY activities are arranged in a logical, developmental sequence and are suitable therefore, without any significant degree of modification, for any child with mild/moderate learning difficulties. This is because SALLEY uses many teaching approaches already familiar in the context of special

education, for example, multi-sensory learning, visual referents and errorless learning.

Application has shown that this group of children manages well in the mainstream nursery SALLEY groups. Individual children can also benefit. Children with learning difficulties are increasingly educated within mainstream settings and schools are required to meet their particular needs through individual education plans, many of which will identify early reading skills as key targets. SALLEY can be used with these children. What they may need is more exposure to the programme and repetition. The teacher will need high expectations as this has a significant effect on outcome (Hurd and McQueen, 2001) and must be prepared to differentiate the activities.

If the SALLEY group contains children with a particularly short span of attention it may be worth considering whether to reduce the size of the group, thus minimising the time when these particular group members are not actively engaged in the tasks.

There are no hard and fast rules to apply here, but all children can benefit by having help with the development of attention, memory, sequencing, listening, and discrimination (the core skills see page 19).

SALLEY has also been used successfully with children with severe learning difficulties. Both group and individual work have been found to have very positive outcomes in terms of the development of phonological awareness skills.

Twenty or so years ago it was thought unimportant to teach children with severe learning difficulties to read. The limit of their exposure to text was social sight vocabulary. However the joy and value of being literate is now introduced to **all** children.

Phonological awareness is equally important when teaching children with severe learning difficulties and interestingly many aspects of the programme were learned with ease. LePrevost (1999) initially taught sounds with visual referents to babies and toddlers with Down's Syndrome. It has proved equally possible to teach Down's babies from 12 months old for example, all the initial grapheme/phoneme correspondences found in SALLEY as part of an early intervention programme.

In addition, group work with pupils at a school for children with severe learning difficulties resulted in all the children being able to complete most of the programme but over a longer time-scale than the 100 days. All the children could discriminate phonemes, decode and encode, discriminate rhyme versus no rhyme, clap out syllable structure and identify onsets, for example, by the end of the trial.

Children with English as an additional language
Children whose home language is not English enter Nursery and Reception classes with varying degrees of competence in English. Their parents may or may not speak English at home and some will have older siblings who have a good command of English. Many children will have had exposure to English through the normal media (TV, radio, etc).

Research evidence suggests that being exposed to more than one language may actually heighten the child's sensitivity to the phonological aspects of the language (Bruck and Genesee, 1995). We also know that phonological awareness skills are a significant predictor of later reading achievement irrespective of the child's first language (Muter and Diethelm, 2001). Studies carried out on children speaking Spanish and English as their first and second language, and vice versa, indicated that there was a cross-language transfer of meta-linguistic skills independent of the language of instruction (Carlisle, Beeman, Davis and Sphraim, 1998). Therefore we can assume that, regardless of the language of instruction, children who develop high phonological awareness will acquire reading with greater facility. Phonological awareness in both languages should be equivalent.

For children with English as an additional language:

- the National Curriculum requires all children to acquire literacy skills in English,
- we know that having well developed phonological awareness skills is an important precursor to the successful acquisition of literacy skills and this will be true for a child speaking any language, be it English, Urdu, French, or Russian,
- prior to learning the skills of phoneme/grapheme correspondence and more sophisticated phonological awareness skills, all children will benefit by learning the 'core skills' of attention, listening, discrimination, memory, and sequencing, thus enabling them to learn how to manipulate sounds.

Therefore exposure to SALLEY is entirely appropriate for children with English as an additional language. However, reports from teaching staff in schools where SALLEY has been introduced indicate that where there is a high proportion of pupils with English as an additional language, it is advisable to delay the introduction of SALLEY until the pupils have had a chance to acclimatise to their new environment and the continual use of the English language. We therefore recommend that in these circumstances staff should consider delaying the start of the programme for about a term after the pupil's entry to school.

Children with specific literacy difficulties

There is some debate about the terminology in this area. However, the term 'specific literacy difficulty' is often considered to be synonymous with dyslexia. Snowling and Stackhouse (1996) define it as "children who are reading significantly below the expected level, or who have unexpected reading difficulties".

Most dyslexic children are identified when they have actually failed to learn to read. Interestingly, one of the most pervasive features found in adults with dyslexia is "persistent difficulties with phonological awareness" (Bruck, 1990).

SALLEY has been successfully used to tackle phonological awareness with individuals and small groups with dyslexia. As the children were older (around 6 years plus), there was less emphasis placed on the core skills, but more repetition, revision and time spent on the fundamental skills of onset identification, knowledge of rhyme and syllable segmentation.

It is still advisable to follow the developmental progression of the programme, and to use the key teaching principles, particularly the multi-sensory approach.

SALLEY has a number of features which are beneficial when teaching children with dyslexia. These include: the multi-sensory teaching approach, recurrent themes, providing opportunities for over learning, a highly structured approach which is strong on the development of phonics, and a sequential and cumulative approach to teaching generally. Perhaps most important, however, is that learning with SALLEY is fun. Older children too, equally enjoy the rhymes which conclude the later daily programmes, the physical movement, and the SALLEY puppet.

THE EVIDENCE BASE

How did we begin?

During an informal discussion, it was agreed that if it was possible to increase a child's language proficiency during the pre-school years then we might expect that scores in literacy skills, at least at the end of Key Stage 1, would be improved. We agreed that there were many factors responsible for the children's low language levels, many of which were not within our control.

Locke et al (2002) found that "it is clear that more children from economically deprived backgrounds enter nursery school with marked language delay". This was clearly the case in Sandwell.

It was acknowledged that, at that time, working with families prior to school entry would be desirable but was unlikely to be effective for us due to difficulties of access, continuity, and the enormity of such an undertaking. The effects of low income, poor housing, and a generally deprived economic landscape were factors over which we had no influence. What we were clear about was that any form of long term intervention programme would need to be within our control if we were to be able to measure its effectiveness with any degree of confidence. The only reliable way to do this was to administer a programme within the context of the nursery school.

It was agreed that a research study should be undertaken with the aim of investigating the influence of intervention at the Foundation Stage. If the study showed that, with specific teaching, children's subsequent literacy skills were improved, then the programme would be adopted throughout the authority. The proposal was discussed with senior officers in the authority who agreed that the study would be a worthwhile venture and secured sufficient funding to enable the research to proceed.

Rationale for the study

It was agreed that any programme would need to be implemented as early in the child's life as possible, and that it should be available to all children regardless of prior knowledge. As mentioned in the previous section, it would have been desirable but impracticable for us to work with children and their families prior to their entry to school. It was therefore logical to attempt to begin work with children as soon as they were within the controlled setting of the Foundation Stage. We were also aware that it was too ambitious to simply attempt to improve 'general language skills' during a child's foundation years, with the expectation that this would improve subsequent attainment levels in literacy. We needed to identify cause and effect, i.e. the particular aspects of an intervention programme that were responsible for improved literacy.

Research has highlighted the importance of phonological awareness in the development of literacy skills (Adams, 1990; Goswami and Bryant, 1990). However there is some dispute in the literature. The debate about the role of phonological awareness – whether it is a consequence or a prerequisite of literacy development – came to a head in the '70s and '80s. However it became clear that the relationship was generally "a reciprocal one" (Stackhouse and Wells, 1997). Some specific aspects were identified as being well within the ability range of "normally developing pre-school children". Liberman, Shankweiler, Fischer and Carter (1974) highlighted syllable segmentation tasks, and Stackhouse and Wells (1997) pointed out that young children can also identify initial phonemes in words before they can actually read. The influence of reading continues the process of refining the child's knowledge of word structure, but many of the skills are within the capacity of pre-school children.

One of the major factors in promoting later literacy seems to be the "phonological linkage hypothesis" (Hatcher, Hulme and Ellis, 1994) where children can connect their phonological awareness skills to letter knowledge.

It was therefore agreed that the development of these skills should be the focus of our programme.

Various commercially available programmes were considered but it was felt that none of them appeared to start at a level that would allow all of the children to participate. Many did not address the issue of core skills and many programmes were aimed at an older age group with certain skills already assumed to be in place. It was therefore agreed that we needed to write a programme of our own.

The aim was to produce a programme that met the key principles that we felt were critical for the development of phonological awareness skills in pre-school children (see page 16).

The result is a hundred days of structured teaching, which can be found in the *SALLEY Manual* (Hurd and McQueen, 2002). Following trials, additions and alterations were made in response to participant feedback and the final version was used in the research study.

Methodology

All schools with nursery classes in the Tipton area of Sandwell were invited to a meeting where a rationale and overview of the project were outlined.

Schools were informed that funding for the project had been approved through the Tipton Challenge Board. The project could therefore proceed at no financial cost to the participating schools.

Each participating school was required to:

- allow members of the project team into their school during the forthcoming academic year. There was a need to carry out individual and group testing of participating children at the start and end of the programme. (This was carried out by the research team.)

- release nursery teaching and non-teaching staff for training by the project team (3 full days). This provided information on the theory and rationale for the programme, plus instruction on programme delivery.
- administer the SALLEY programme on a daily basis for 100 days.

Four schools were selected. Whole nursery groups (morning attenders or afternoon attenders) in each school, were assigned to either experimental or control groups. In two of the schools the morning attenders were designated as 'experimental', with the afternoon attenders designated as 'controls'. In the two remaining schools, morning attenders were designated as 'controls' and afternoon attenders as 'experimental'. This allowed us to cancel out any temporal effects. The four schools gave us a total experimental sample of 66 children and 37 controls. All children ranged in age from 3;3 to 4;2.

In each school, research assistants administered individual tests to all children in both experimental and control groups. The following tests were selected:

a) Comprehension section of The Reynell Developmental Language Scales III (Edwards, Fletcher, Garman, Hughes, Letts and Sinka, 1997). This is a well established and proven test of children's receptive language skills. It has 62 items in 11 sections and starts with understanding of single words and ends with inferencing. This samples a wide range of comprehension skills.

b) Picture Similarities subtest of the British Ability Scales II (Elliott, Smith and McCulloch, 1996). This is described as a non-verbal test in that the task involves matching pictures that have a common element or concept. The items are arranged in order of difficulty.

c) Phonological Awareness Assessment Test (Hurd and McQueen, 1998). This test looks in detail at all the areas subsequently taught in the SALLEY programme including core skills, key language concepts, initial letter sounds, end sound identification, sound blending and rhyming.

All nursery staff received training about the theory, rationale, and administration of the programme (a two-day course followed by two half days later in the year).

To enable us to look at the progress of children's phonological awareness skills in nurseries where there had been no exposure to the SALLEY programme, two additional schools were selected in the same catchment area.

Thus, in effect we had a second control group (control 2s) consisting of a total of 56 pupils. This second control group would, of course, have exposure to a different educational environment to the children in the four original schools.

Prior to the start of the SALLEY programme, it was necessary to carry out individual testing of all the children in the study (experimentals and control groups 1 and 2), followed by a statistical analysis of the test scores to confirm or otherwise that we had experimental and control groups that could be considered to have comparable verbal skills, non-verbal skills, and phonological awareness skills.

Once the baseline testing was completed the schools began delivering the SALLEY programme.

At the end of the programme delivery, the Phonological Awareness Test (Hurd and McQueen, 1998) was administered blindly a second time to all the children, to measure their phonological awareness skills.

The population in Tipton is largely white and monolingual. In view of the multi-ethnic makeup of the local authority, we wanted to obtain information about how the programme could assist children with English as an additional language. It was decided that a second cohort of four schools in the Smethwick area of Sandwell be invited to take part in the project. The essential difference between the cohorts in Tipton and Smethwick was that the Smethwick cohort was in an area where there was a high ethnic minority population.

The breakdown by ethnicity of the Smethwick cohort was as follows:

White	15%
Black/Caribbean	1.25%
Bangladeshi	17.5%
Pakistani	22.5%
Indian	23.75%
Sikh	13.75%
Other	6.25%
Total	100%

We felt that there was no reason why phonological awareness skills should not be taught to children from ethnic minority backgrounds. The programme delivery in Smethwick was exactly the same as in Tipton, except that the British Picture Vocabulary Scales (B.P.V.S) (Dunn, Dunn, Whetton and Burley, 1997) were administered as an additional baseline test to the Smethwick children. This extra pre-SALLEY test was to ensure that the control and experimental groups in Smethwick could be considered to have an equivalent facility with English at the start of the programme.

There were 40 experimental children and 38 control group children, ranging in age from 3;3 to 4;3.

Results

Tipton – pre-SALLEY
The three groups (experimental, control 1 and control 2)
had equal numbers of boys and girls in each, and each group
had the same mean age.
The sample size was as follows:

Group	Number of subjects
Experimental	**66**
Control 1	**37**
Control 2	**56**

At the start of the study we were concerned to establish
the homogeneity of our sample, thus enabling us to conclude
that any post-programme differences in phonological skills
could be attributed to SALLEY.

Each of the individual tests, i.e. Picture Similarities from
the British Ability Scales (B.A.S) (Elliott et al, 1996), Reynell
Developmental Language Scales III comprehension (Edwards
et al, 1997) and the Phonological Awareness Test (Hurd and
McQueen, 1998), were administered to the three groups
(experimental, control 1 and control 2).

We compared the mean difference between three groups
on each test using a one way analysis of variance.

The ANOVA (Table 1) shows that there was no significant
difference at 0.05 level between the groups of test scores.
Therefore the experimental and controls 1 and 2 could be
regarded as performing equally on the Picture Similarities
test (Elliott et al, 1996).

Table 1

Table to show ANCVA for the pre-SALLEY Picture Similarities test (from the British Ability Scales II) (Elliott et al, 1996)

	N	Mean	Std Dev	Std Error	95% Confidence Interval for Mean	
					Lower Bound	Upper Bound
Experimental	66	49.82	6.53	80	48.21	51.42
Control 1	37	49.3	8.61	1.42	46.43	52.17
Control 2	56	47.79	7.24	0.97	45.85	49.72
Total	159	48.98	7.31	0.58	47.84	50.13

	Sum of Squares	DF	Mean Square	F	Sig
Between groups	129.967	2	64.983	1.218	.299
Within groups	8322.97	156	53.352		
Total	8452.94	158			

The ANOVA (Table 2) shows that there was no significant difference at the 0.05 level between the groups of test scores. Therefore the experimental and controls 1 and 2 could be regarded as performing equally on the Reynell Developmental Language Scales comprehension test (Edwards et al, 1997).

Table 2
Table to show ANOVA for the pre-SALLEY Reynell Developmental Language Scales III comprehension test (Edwards et al, 1997)

	N	Mean	Std Dev	Std Error	95% Confidence Interval for Mean	
					Lower Bound	Upper Bound
Experimental	66	43.13	14.06	1.68	39.79	46.49
Control 1	37	43.6	12.68	1.96	39.64	47.55
Control 2	56	46.96	11.44	1.34	44.29	49.63
Total	159	44.75	12.82	0.94	42.89	46.61

	Sum of Squares	DF	Mean Square	F	Sig
Between groups	592.995	2	296.497	1.821	.165
Within groups	29639.6	182	162.855		
Total	30232.6	184			

The ANOVA (Table 3) shows that there was no significant difference at the 0.05 level between the groups of test scores. Therefore the experimental and controls 1 and 2 could be regarded as performing equally on the Phonological Awareness Test (Hurd and McQueen, 1998).

Table 3

Table to show ANOVA for the pre-SALLEY Phonological Awareness Test (Hurd and McQueen, 1998)

	N	Mean	Std Dev	Std Error	95% Confidence Interval for Mean Lower Bound	Upper Bound
Experimental	66	21.55	16.18	1.99	17.57	25.52
Control 1	37	19.59	8.49	1.40	16.76	22.43
Control 2	56	21.11	11.01	1.47	18.16	24.05
Total	159	20394	12.92	1.02	18.91	22.96

	Sum of Squares	DF	Mean Square	F	Sig
Between groups	92.731	2	296	1.821	.165
Within groups	26266.6	156	162.855		
Total	26359.3	158			

None of the tests showed any significant difference between the groups at the 0.05 level of significance.

The results confirmed that at the beginning of the project we were dealing with three groups of children (experimental, control 1 and control 2) that could be considered to be at the same starting point as measured by the non-verbal, verbal, and phonological awareness tests.

Tipton – post-SALLEY

At the start of the programme the statistical analysis of the three tests established that there was no significant difference in the mean scores of the three groups. At the end of the delivery of SALLEY to the experimental group, all the children in the three groups were given the Phonological Awareness Test (Hurd and McQueen, 1998) for a second time.

Again we were dealing with three sets of data and wanted to compare the mean score of each. An analysis of variance (ANOVA) was carried out to compare the post-SALLEY scores of the experimental and control groups. This would inform us whether there was any difference between the mean scores for the three groups (Table 4).

Table 4

Table to show ANOVA for the post-SALLEY Phonological Awareness Test (Hurd and McQueen, 1998)

	N	Mean	Std Dev	Std Error	95% Confidence Interval for Mean	
					Lower Bound	Upper Bound
Experimental	66	56.36	38.50	4.74	46.9	65.83
Control 1	37	35.89	31.43	5.17	25.41	46.37
Control 2	56	31.21	18.83	2.52	26.17	36.26
Total	159	42.74	33.07	2.62	37.56	47.92

	Sum of Squares	DF	Mean Square	F	Sig
Between groups	21424.2	2	10712.079	11.04	.000
Within groups	151406.3	156	970.553		
Total	172830.4	158			

The ANOVA showed that there was a significant difference in the scores of the three groups, but it did not show between which groups the difference lay. It was therefore necessary to carry out a test of multiple comparisons (a post hoc test) (Table 5).

Table 5

Multiple Comparisons Test (Scheffe) for the post-SALLEY Phonological Awareness Test (Hurd and McQueen, 1998)

Group	N	Subset for alpha = 0.05	
		1	2
Control 2	56	31.21	
Control 1	37	35.89	
Experimental	66		56.36
Sig		.755	1.000

Group	Group	Mean Diff (I – J)	Std Error	Signif	95% Confidence Interval for Mean	
					Lower Bound	Upper Bound
Experimental	Control 1	20.47*	6.40	.007	4.66	36.28
	Control 2	25.15*	5.66	.000	11.16	39.14
Control 1	Experimental	-20.47*	6.40	.007	-36.28	-4.66
	Control 2	4.68	6.40	.778	-11.63	20.99
Control 2	Experimental	-25.15	5.66	.000	-39.14	-11.16
	Control 1	-4.68	6.60	.778	-20.99	11.16

* the mean difference is significant at the 0.05 level

The Multiple Comparisons Test (Scheffe) demonstrated that control 1 and control 2 formed a homogenous subset. Therefore the significant differences existed between control 1 and experimental and between control 2 and experimental. There was no significant difference between the two control groups.

We were now able to conclude that, although all three groups (experimental, control 1 and control 2) had increased their mean scores on the Phonological Awareness Test (Hurd and McQueen, 1998), those children who had been exposed to the SALLEY programme (experimentals) had improved their mean scores to such a degree that they were statistically significantly better than the other two groups (control 1 and 2) at the finish of the programme (see Figure 1).

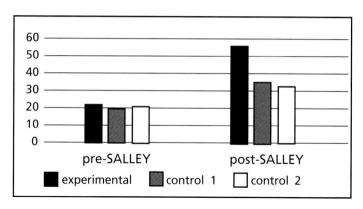

Figure 1 A graph to show the mean scores in the Phonological Awareness Test in Tipton.

Smethwick – pre-SALLEY

The make up of the total sample was 85% Asian and 15% white monolingual.

The sample size was as follows:

Group	Number of subjects
Experimental	**40**
Control	**38**

The groups were equally populated with boys and girls and there was no statistical difference in mean age. Each of the four Smethwick schools had morning and afternoon teaching groups. Two schools had their experimental group in the morning and control group in the afternoon, and two had controls in the morning and experimentals in the afternoon.

In view of the results in Tipton, that showed no difference in the performance of the two sets of control groups (control 1s in the same schools as the experimental groups and control 2s in completely separate schools), it was considered unnecessary to have a second set of control groups.

As with the Tipton sample, we were keen to establish the homogeneity between the groups prior to the delivery of SALLEY. The same set of tests was administered to the Smethwick children as for the Tipton group: Picture Similarities from the British Ability Scales (Elliott et al, 1996), Reynell Developmental Language Scales III comprehension (Edwards et al, 1997) and the Phonological Awareness Test (Hurd and McQueen, 1998). But a further test of listening vocabulary, the British Picture Vocabulary Scales (B.P.V.S) (Dunn, Dunn, Whetton and Burley, 1997), was added because of the possible variations in the children's facility with English.

For each of the four pre-SALLEY tests we needed to establish that the groups were equal at the start of the programme. We therefore needed to compare the mean scores of the experimental group and the control group on each of the four tests. We were dealing with two groups and it was therefore appropriate to use a t-test for independent samples (see Tables

6, 7, 8 and 9). The results indicated that there was no significant difference between the scores for the experimental group and the control group on each of the four tests and we could therefore assume that the two groups could be considered to be equal at the start of the programme.

Table 6

T-test of pre-SALLEY B.P.V.S (Dunn, Dunn, Whetton and Burley, 1997) Smethwick

Group statistics

Group		N	Mean	Std Dev	Std Error Mean
STSCORE	Experimental	40	79.75	16.87	2.67
	Control	38	75.05	18.57	3.01

		Levene's Test for Equality of Variances	
		F	SIG
STSCORE	Equal variances assumed	1.847	.178
	Equal variances not assumed		

		T-test for Equality of Means			
		T	DF	SIG (2 Tailed)	Mean Difference
STSCORE	Equal variances assumed	1.170	76	.246	4.70
	Equal variances not assumed	1.167	74.387	.247	4.70

		T-test for Equality of Means		
		Std Error Difference	95% Confidence Interval of the Difference Lower	Upper
STSCORE	Equal variances assumed	4.01	-3.30	12.69
	Equal variances not assumed	4.02	-3.32	12.71

Table 7

T-test for pre-SALLEY Picture Similarities Test (from the British Ability Scales II) (Elliott et al, 1996)

Group		N	Mean	Std Dev	Std Error Mean
TSCORE	Experimental	40	42.60	9.02	1.43
	Control	38	44.84	7.59	1.23

		Levene's Test for Equality of Variances	
		F	SIG
TSCORE	Equal variances assumed		
	Equal variances not assumed	.116	.734

Table 8

Pre-SALLEY Reynell Developmental Language Scales III (Edwards et al, 1997) Ref Scores (Smethwick)

Group		N	Mean	Std Dev	Std Error Mean
STSCORE	Experimental	40	32.70	19.22	3.04
	Control	37	31.35	19.67	3.23

		Levene's Test for Equality of Variances	
		F	Sig
STSCORE	Equal variances assumed	.073	.788
	Equal variances not assumed		

		T-test for Equality of Means			
		T	DF	Sig (2 Tailed)	Mean Difference
STSCORE	Equal variances assumed	.304	75	.762	1.35
	Equal variances not assumed	.304	74.230	.762	1.35

		T-test for Equality of Means		
		Std Error Difference	95% Confidence Interval of the Difference	
			Lower	Upper
STSCORE	Equal variances assumed	4.43	-7.48	10.18
	Equal variances not assumed	4.44	-7.49	10.19

Table 9

T-test for pre-SALLEY Phonological Awarenes Test (Hurd and McQueen, 1998) Smethwick

	N	Mean	Std Dev	Std Error	95% Confidence Interval for Mean	
					Lower Bound	Upper Bound
Experimental	39	11.23	10.33	1.65	7.88	14.58
Control	40	12.43	8.41	1.33	9.74	15.11
Total	79	11.84	9.37	1.05	9.74	13.93

	Minimum	Maximum
Experimental	0	55
Control	1	39
Total	0	55

Levene Statistic	DF1	DF2	Sig
171	1	77	.681

	Sum of Squares	DF	Mean Square	F	Sig
Between groups	28.163	1	28.163	.318	.574
Within groups	6812.698	77	88.477		
Total	6840.861	78			

Smethwick – post-SALLEY

At the end of the programme delivery, both the experimental and control group were re-tested on the Phonological Awareness Test (Hurd and McQueen, 1998) (see Table 10). The results were analysed (using a t-test for independent samples) and showed that at the end of the programme the experimental group achieved a mean score that was higher than that achieved by the control group, and the difference was statistically significant at the 0.01 level.

Table 10

Table to show t-test for post-SALLEY Phonological Awareness Test (Hurd and McQueen, 1998)

Group	Means	Equal Variance?	Level of Significance
Experimental	59.58	YES	0.009
Control	39.94		

Looking qualitatively at the data, the most significant differences between the experimentals and the controls were found in the areas of:

- key language concepts,
- syllable clapping,
- rhyme identification, both silent and spoken,
- initial letter sound identification (spoken),
- initial letter sound (silent), and
- real and non-word discrimination.

Indicative key areas of the intervention programme had a statistically significant impact on the children's learning. Interestingly, the least significant area was more complex blending, which had least emphasis at the end of the programme.

From the graph (Figure 2) it can be seen that the results indicated that although the 2 groups had both increased their mean scores on the Phonological Awareness Test (Hurd and McQueen, 1998), those children who had been exposed to the SALLEY programme (experimental) had increased their mean scores to such a degree that they were statistically significantly better than the controls at the 0.01 level.

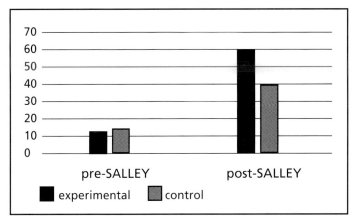

Figure 2 A graph to show the mean scores in the Phonological Awareness Test in Smethwick.

At the end of the programme practitioners in the eight participating nurseries were asked to anonymously complete a questionnaire about the programme. Forty three questionnaires were returned. Responses indicated that:

- 97% thought that SALLEY children were better at listening and responding to teacher instructions than non-SALLEY children,

- 60% considered the SALLEY children were better behaved than the non-SALLEY children,

- 55% said that SALLEY children were more able to attend during whole-class activities,

- 78% felt SALLEY children were making better progress in literacy then non-SALLEY children,

- 86% considered that SALLEY should continue to be delivered in the nursery class at their school, and

- 84% considered that SALLEY should be delivered in the Reception class at their school.

Hurd and McQueen (2001) also looked at the impact of teacher expectations. Semi-structured interviews were conducted. These were held to gain staff views before and after the study, followed by individual interviews with the staff who had been involved in the study (group based). The results showed that expectation of outcome was highly correlated with the children's outcomes as measured by the Phonological Awareness Test (Hurd and McQueen, 1998). This also has significant implications for the implementation of programmes like SALLEY. Those staff, for example, who felt that the children were not capable of achieving such a range of phonological awareness skills actually had children who scored lower final measure outcomes than those who had higher expectations.

Conclusions and implications

The results of both the Tipton and Smethwick cohorts indicated that at the end of the programme the pupils that had participated in the SALLEY programme performed significantly better on the Phonological Awareness Test (Hurd and McQueen, 1998) than the control groups.

The SALLEY programme had been shown to be effective in developing phonological awareness with all children regardless of their ethnic background, their skill levels on entry to nursery class, and previous experience. Research evidence links phonological awareness and future reading success, and we suggest that the children who received the SALLEY programme will be advantaged in their acquisition of reading skills. Access to the National Curriculum is highly dependent on literacy skills, and we therefore predict that the children who have received SALLEY will be better equipped to take advantage of the National Curriculum.

At the time of writing, we have no hard evidence about the subsequent reading skills of the participant pupils as all the pupils are still at Key Stage 1. A further intended development of the research is to follow this group of children through their school careers and to measure their reading skills at key points (possibly as an add-on to SATs).

It is evident from the results that phonological awareness skills can be greatly enhanced by specific intervention, in the pre-school population. What was most important for the practitioners involved was that the programme offered a structured, daily intervention that could be carried out by any number of staff. This gave benefits for all. The children responded positively to the group-based activities and seemed to enjoy their SALLEY sessions.

The staff also felt that they could see the children making progress before their eyes, and that the repetition and recurrent themes meant that all children could benefit. In addition, staff praised the use of any language concepts. This enabled staff and children alike to have a common vocabulary to talk about language. But perhaps most of all, everyone felt the programme made learning fun!

HOW MIGHT RESOURCES BE USED MORE EFFECTIVELY?

SALLEY research monies were available for two specific geographical areas only. However, an additional nursery in another part of the borough expressed interest in the project. This nursery was sufficiently committed to fund the training, and has continued to deliver the SALLEY programme as specified in the manual. This nursery is attached to a mainstream primary school, which has an Enhanced Learning Provision (ELP) for children with specific speech and language problems.

The ELP is served by 1.4 whole-time equivalent (WTE) speech and language therapists and was, therefore, the ideal environment for considering the programme as part of a continuum of intervention for children who may be 'at risk' for future literacy acquisition.

Would children who had received SALLEY in the nursery require less additional 'recovery' intervention later?

The Key Stage 1 therapist put in place the following:

- when children were assessed using the Pre-school Indicators in Primary schools (PIPs), on entry into Reception, an extra assessment of phonological awareness skills was added.

This was based on the North and Parker (1993) assessment, which was already in use in the nursery, alongside an additional test for the key language concepts identified as important in the SALLEY programme.

The phonological add-on included:

- syllable awareness,
- onsets,
- rhyming, and
- phoneme-grapheme correspondence.

Following these assessments, the children identified as experiencing difficulties were placed in 'recovery' groups. Their progress was closely monitored.

Additional help required was divided into the following areas:

- help in all areas,
- help in some areas, or
- no additional help required.

In September 1999, 26% of children entering Reception required no additional help. There had been no SALLEY programme running in the nursery at this time.

In September 2000, a mix of SALLEY and non-SALLEY children entered Reception. 35% of the SALLEY children required no additional help. None of the non-SALLEY children fell into this category – all of them were very weak in the area of phonological awareness and this had major implications for the Reception curriculum.

In October 2000, the 'add on' phonological awareness screen was undertaken as part of the baseline assessment carried out on all children entering the nursery. This was prior to the start of SALLEY with these children.

This screen was then carried out again in July 2001.

Most children started with a very low level of phonological awareness skills.

All children made progress with the acquisition of phonological awareness skills over the year because of the specially targeted recovery groups. On entry into Reception, most children reached what was deemed to be an acceptable/

average level of phonological awareness skills for their age.

Again, the children who did not reach the required level to ensure trouble-free development of literacy skills were put on an 'at risk' list and targeted for extra literacy help.

By identifying problem areas earlier, practitioners can ensure effective direction of resources towards the establishment of early 'recovery' strategies. SALLEY suggests that assessment pre- and post-recovery interventions may help to identify persistent and continuing difficulties, and ultimately, where expensive and time-consuming dyslexia assessment might most usefully be considered.

Practitioners wishing to pursue this approach are invited to:

- introduce an 'add-on' for phonological awareness skills in conjunction with nursery baseline assessments or PIPs,
- establish recovery groups as required,
- re-assess at regular intervals,
- identify where persistent difficulties lie, and
- consider looking more closely at this group using a tool such as Cognitive Profiling System (COPs) (Singleton, 1996).

A useful extension of SALLEY has been its use with older, Reception-plus aged children. It has proved to be just as effective, and has enabled children who did not attend a SALLEY nursery to have access to the benefits of the programme. Using it with older children, who had poorly developed phonological awareness skills, gave them a much greater chance of success in the literacy hour. It is interesting to note that the age of introduction is less important than the learning needs of the individual child.

HOW MIGHT WE EARLIER IDENTIFY CHILDREN POTENTIALLY 'AT RISK' OF DYSLEXIA?

During the course of the original research project, all the pre- and post-intervention testing scores were examined and their profiles closely monitored. The researchers looked (post-programme) at the gains made by individual children on the Phonological Awareness Test (Hurd and McQueen, 1998). Gains in phonological awareness skills were plotted against the original profiles for both performance, as measured on the Picture Similarities test of the B.A.S (Elliot et al, 1996), and language skills, as measured on the Reynell Developmental Language Scales (Edwards et al, 1997). There were several children who failed to make significant gains in phonological awareness and we explored the reasons for this. The researchers discounted children with a profile indicative of overall developmental delay and concentrated on those who initially had a mismatch between their performance and language scores.

Five children were identified as having made minimal gains with phonological awareness skills following their participation in SALLEY. These warranted further investigation. These five children were subsequently followed up and assessed using the COPs (Singleton, 1996). The results were extremely interesting.

Individual profiles				
child	lang	perf	risk/concern visual	auditory
female A	↑	↑	✓	
female K	–	↓	✓	
male G	↓	–	✓	
male J	↓	–	✓	✓
female L	↓	–	✓	✓

The arrows indicate above/below average scores compared with chronological age. The ticks indicate risk/concern in visual/auditory areas.

- Three children (6%) had profiles which caused some concern.

- Two children (3%) had profiles which caused particular concern.

An interesting correlation might be made with figures available from the British Dyslexia Association which identified 4% of the population as being severely dyslexic with a further 6% experiencing mild to moderate problems (www.bda-dyslexia.org.uk).

The numbers identified here mirror the numbers expected in the general population. It could be concluded that an additional benefit of SALLEY is that children who are potentially at risk for dyslexia could be identified earlier and resources could be put in place before the problem becomes long term and entrenched (Hurd and McQueen, 2001). It also allows identification before children experience failure in the acquisition of literacy.

WILL SALLEY HELP CHILDREN WHOSE SPEECH IS DIFFICULT TO UNDERSTAND?

When the original research was undertaken, teachers were asked to list children on the programme whom they thought had 'unintelligible' speech.

The thinking behind this was that, although SALLEY is primarily an input programme, in the normal course of events there could potentially be output benefits. This follows the traditional speech and language approach.

From the original study of 160 children, nursery staff identified 58 children whose speech was deemed to be 'unintelligible'.

An independent researcher assessed these children, using the Edinburgh Articulation Test (Anthony, Bogle and Ingram, 1971). This test was selected because it is the only standardised norm referenced speech output assessment.

Of the original 58 children, 34 were found to be within normal limits for their age.

Twenty-four were found to have speech output problems as determined by the Edinburgh Articulation Test (Anthony et al, 1971). The authors followed these children through the SALLEY programme. Twelve were part of the experimental group, and 12 part of the control group.

All these children had also been assessed on the Phonological Awareness Test (Hurd and McQueen, 1998) and prior to the implementation of the SALLEY programme there was no significant difference between the groups as determined by a t-test for independent samples.

After the experimental group had received the SALLEY programme, all the children were re-assessed.

Using the Phonological Awareness Test (Hurd and McQueen, 1998):

- The experimental group made gains which were statistically significant as measured by the Wilcoxon Test (one tailed).
- The control group did not.

Using the Edinburgh Articulation Test (Anthony et al, 1971):

- Both groups had made gains.

Therefore, the authors found that phonological awareness ability was **not** a significant predictor of articulatory age.

So why was this?

The key question appears to be around a diagnostic model, which will be familiar to all speech and language therapists reading this handbook.

Leitae, Hogben and Fletcher (1997) report no relationship between articulation scores and phonological awareness, but they did subsequently identify subgroups of children who had speech output problems that were:

- delayed,
- deviant consistent, or
- deviant inconsistent (poor phonological awareness skills).

It could be hypothesised, therefore, that the speech output difficulties of children identified within the third group may benefit from SALLEY.

For any child with a speech output problem, the level of breakdown is of paramount importance. It is a salutary lesson that a blanket approach to speech output problems is not the answer. It is important to establish the level of breakdown and direct intervention to the specific needs of the individual.

WHAT NEXT?

In this *Handbook* we have given you the philosophy behind the SALLEY programme. We have also presented the results of our original research, showing that children exposed to SALLEY make significant gains in phonological awareness. This persuasive evidence indicates that the programme is effective in equipping children to successfully embark on the National Literacy Strategy.

So, what should you do next? We recommend that you watch the SALLEY video to give you a 'feel' for the programme. You should also read the *Manual,* which will provide you with everything you need to get started.

We hope that you and the children you are working with enjoy the programme. Introduce them to Salley squirrel, teach them good sitting and good listening – and above all, remember to have fun!

DEFINITION OF TERMS

Attention: the ability to focus on a task.

Concentration: sustained attention on a task.

Concept: an idea represented by a specific vocabulary item.

Core (skill): the central or most important part.

Decode: to translate the visual code of letters into a word, i.e. read.

Discrimination: the ability to distinguish between sounds.

Encode: to build up a visual code of letters into a word, i.e. spell.

Grapheme: written representation of a sound, which may consist of one or more letters.

Linguistic: of, or relating to, language or linguistics.

Listening: the ability to hear and process what is heard.

Memory (auditory, visual, kinaesthetic): the ability to recall learned items.

Phonological awareness: the ability to reflect on and manipulate the structure of an utterance as distinct from its meaning.

Phoneme: the smallest unit of sound in a word.

Practitioners: any adults who work in pre-school settings, whatever their qualifications.

Recurrent themes: ideas/subjects which are cyclically re-visited.

Rhyme: words containing the same rime in their final syllable (as defined by the NLS).

Rime: that part of a syllable which contains the vowel and final consonant (cluster) (if there is one).

Sequencing: the ability to do a task in a given order.

Setting: local authority nurseries, playgroups, pre-schools, child-minders – any pre-school provision including specialist language units, special schools and health-run nurseries.

Syllable: each beat in a word is a syllable.

Visual referent: the tangible representation of an abstract concept.

REFERENCES

Abudarham, S., (2002) 'Early Intervention' in Abudarham, S., and Hurd, A., (2002) *Management of Communication Needs in People with Learning Disability*. Whurr, London.

Adams, M., (1990) *Beginning to read and learning to think about print*. Cambridge MIT Press, Cambridge.

Anthony, A., Bogle, D., and Ingram, T., (1971) *The Edinburgh Articulation Test*. E & S Livingstone, Edinburgh.

Bishop, D., (1997) *Uncommon Understanding*. Psychology Press, Cambridge.

Bradley, L., and Bryant, E., (1985) Rhyme and reason in reading and spelling. *IARLD Monograph No.1*. Ann Arbour, University of Michigan, USA.

Bradley, L., (1988) Making connections in learning to read and spell. *Applied Cognitive Psychology* 2: 3–18.

Bruck, M., (1990) Persistence of dyslexics phonological awareness deficits. *Developmental Psychology* 28: 874–886.

Bruck, M., and Genesee, F., (1995) Phonological Awareness in Young Second Language Learners. *Journal of Child Language* 22: 307–324.

Carlisle, J.F., Beeman, M., Davis, K.H., and Sphraim, G., (1998) Relationships of meta-linguistic capabilities and reading achievement for children who are becoming bilingual. Paper presented to the Fifth Annual Meeting of the Society for the Scientific Study of Reading. San Diego, CA, USA.

Chiappe, P., and Siegel, L., (1999) Phonological Awareness and Reading Acquisition in English and Punjabi Speaking Canadian Children. *Journal of Educational Psychology* 91 (1): 20–28.

Cooper, J., Moodley, M., and Reynell, J., (1978) *Helping Children's Language Development.* Edward Arnold, London.

Dean, E., Howell, J., Hill, A., and Waters, D., (1990) *Metaphon Resource Pack.* NFER Nelson, London.
DfEE (2000) *Curriculum Guidance for the Foundation Stage.* The Qualifications and Curriculum Authority, London.
DfEE (1998) *National Literacy Strategy.* Department for Education and Employment, London.
Dunn, L., Dunn, L., Whetton, C., and Burley, J., (1997) *British Picture Vocabulary Scales, Second Edition.* NFER Nelson, London.

Edwards, S., Fletcher, P., Garman, M., Hughes, A., Letts, C., and Sinka, I., (1997) *The Reynell Developmental Language Scales III.* NFER Nelson, London.
Elliott, C., Smith, P., and McCulloch, K., (1996) *British Ability Scales II.* NFER Nelson, London.
Ellis, A., (1991) *Reading, Writing and Dyslexia; A Cognitive Analysis.* Open University Press, Milton Keynes.

Goswami, U., and Bryant, P., (1990) *Phonological Skills and Learning to Read.* Hove, Laumen and Erlbaum, New York, USA.

Hatcher, P., Hulme, C., and Ellis, A., (1994) Ameliorating early reading failure by integrating the teaching of reading and phonological skills. The Phonological Linkage Hypothesis. *Child Development* 65: 41–57.
Heckerman, K., Alber, S., Hooper, S., and Heward, W., (1998) A comparison of least to most and progressive time delay on the disruptive behaviour of students with Autism. *Journal of Behavioural Education* 8: 171–202.

Hurd, A., and McQueen, D., (2001) The Impact of Teacher Expectations. Paper presented at the Royal College of Speech and Language Therapists' (R.C.S.L.T) Conference, Birmingham.

Hurd, A., and McQueen, D., (2001) Whose children? Paper presented at the R.C.S.L.T Conference, Birmingham.

Hurd, A., and McQueen, D., (2001) How might we identify children at risk for dyslexia? Paper presented at the British Dyslexia Association National Conference, York.

Hurd, A., and McQueen, D., (2000) Phonological awareness training as an indirect therapy for phonological disorders. CPLOL Conference, Paris, France.

Hurd, A., and McQueen, D., (1998) *Phonological Awareness Test*. Training Material – Sandwell Healthcare NHS Trust.

Karnes, M., and Lee, R., (1978) *Early Childhood*. The Council for Exceptional Children, Reston, VA, USA.

Layton, L., and Deeny, K., (1996) 'Promoting Phonological Awareness in Pre School Children' in Snowling, M., and Stackhouse, J., (1996) *Dyslexia, Speech and Language*. Whurr, London.

Leitae, S., Hogben, J., and Fletcher, J., (1997) Phonological Processing Skills in Speech and Language Impaired Children. *European Journal of Disorders of Communication* 32: 73–93.

LeProvost, P., (1999) in Buckley, S., (1999) 'Promoting the Cognitive Development of Children with Down's Syndrome. The Practical Implications of Recent Research' in Rondal, J.A., Perera, J., and Nadel, L., (eds) *Down's Syndrome – a review of current knowledge*. Whurr, London.

Liberman, I., Shankweiler, D., Fischer, F., and Carter, B., (1974) Reading and the awareness of linguistic segments. *Journal of Experimental Child Psychology* 18: 201–12.

Light, P., Remington, B., Clarke, S., and Watson, J., (1989) in Beveridge, M., Conti-Ramsden, G., and Leudar, I., *Language and Communication in Mentally Handicapped People*. Chapman-Hall, London.

Locke, A., Ginsborg, J., and Peers, I., (2002) Development and Disadvantage – Implications for Early Years and Beyond. *I.J.L.C.D* Vol 37, No. 1, 3–17.

Lundberg, I., Frost, J., and Peterson, O., (1988) Effects of an extensive programme for stimulating phonological awareness in pre school children. *Reading Research Quarterly* 23: 263–84.

Maclean, M., Bryant, P., and Bradley, L., (1987) Rhymes, nursery rhymes and reading in early childhood. *Merrill Palmer Quarterly* 33: 255–81.

Masterson, J., Hazan, V., and Wijayatilake, l., (1995) Phonemic processing problems in developmental phonological dyslexia. *Cognitive Neuropsychology* 12: 3 233–259.

McQueen, D., (1999) Research in Progress. Paper presented at R.C.S.L.T regional study day, Oldbury.

Merzenich, M., Jenkins, W., Schreiner, C., Miller, S.L., Tallal, P., and Johnston, P., (1996) Temporal processing deficits of language impaired children ameliorated by trauma. *Science* 271: 77–81.

Muter, V., and Diethelm, K., (2001) The Contribution of Phonological Skills and Letter Knowledge to Early Reading Development in a Multilingual Population. *Language Learning* 51.2 June 2001, pp. 187–219.

North, C., and Parker, M., (1993) *Phonological Awareness Assessment*. Available from Clare North, Downside Cottage, Summerhill, Althorne, Essex CM3 6BY.

Ofsted (1998) *The Quality of Education in Institutions Inspected under the Nursery Education Funding Arrangement.* Ofsted, London.

Perfetti, C., Bell, L., Beck, I., and Hughes, C., (1987) Phonemic knowledge and learning to read are reciprocal – a longitudinal study of first grade children. *Merrill Palmer Quarterly* 33: 283–319.
Performance Indicators in Primary Schools (1999) University of Durham.

Rondal, J.A., Perera, J., and Nadel, L., (eds) (1999) *Down's Syndrome – a review of current knowledge.* Whurr, London.
Reid, G., (1998) *Dyslexia – a practitioners handbook.* Wiley Eveland, England.
R.C.S.L.T (1996) *Communicating Quality 2.* London.

Singleton, C.H., Horne, J.K., and Thomas, K.V., (1999) Computerised Baseline Assessment of Literacy. *Journal of Research in Reading* 22: pp. 67–80.
Singleton, C., (1996) *Cognitive Profiling System.* Chameleon Educational Limited, Nottingham.
Snowling, M., and Stackhouse, J., (1996) *Dyslexia, speech and language.* Whurr, London.
Stackhouse, J., and Wells, B., (1997) *Children's speech and literacy difficulties. A psycholinguistic framework.* Whurr, London.

Tallal, P., (1980) Auditory Temporal Perception. Phonics and reading disability. *Brain and Language* 9: 182–198.
Touchette, P.E., and Howard, J., (1984) Errorless Learning Reinforcement Contingencies and Stimulus Control Transfer in Delayed Prompting. *JABA* 17: 175–181.

Vance, M., (1994) Phonological processing, verbal comprehension and lexical representation. Proceedings of NAPLIC Conference – *Understanding Comprehension*, Birmingham.

Williams, G., (2002) in Abudarham, S., and Hurd, A., (eds) *The Management of Communication Needs in People with Learning Disability*. Whurr, London.

Wray, D., (1994) *Language and Awareness*. Hodder and Stoughton, London.